P9-CRQ-353

What's the Difference?

A Guide to Some Familiar Animal Look-Alikes

What's the Difference?

A Guide to Some Familiar Animal Look-Alikes

BY ELIZABETH A. LACEY

Illustrated by
ROBERT SHETTERLY

CLARION BOOKS · NEW YORK

The author gratefully acknowledges the assistance of
Peter H. Klopfer, Professor of Zoology, Duke University,
in reviewing text and illustrations for accuracy.

Clarion Books
a Houghton Mifflin Company imprint
215 Park Avenue South, New York, NY 10003
Text copyright © 1993 by Elizabeth A. Lacey
Illustrations copyright © 1993 by Robert Shetterly

Library of Congress Cataloging-in-Publication Data

Lacey, Elizabeth A.
What's the difference? : a guide to some familiar animal
look-alikes / Elizabeth A. Lacey ; illustrated by Robert
Shetterly.
p.   cm.
Includes bibliographical references and index.
Summary: Examines the physical and behavioral
similarities and differences between crocodiles and
alligators, hares and rabbits, seals and sea lions, and other
animal look-alikes.
ISBN 0-395-56182-5
1. Animals — Juvenile literature.   2. Zoology —
Nomenclature (Popular) — Juvenile literature.   3. Zoology —
Classification — Juvenile literature.   [1. Animals. 2.
Zoology.]   I. Shetterly, Robert, ill.   II. Title.
QL49.L15   1992   91-15810
591— dc20   CIP   AC

HOR 10 9 8 7 6 5 4 3 2 1

Dedicated to the memory of
Anna A. Behrensmeyer
a good friend and a great lady
"We must cherish the earth . . . and leave all
children a legacy of hope."

Contents

There is always more to learn, and this
is part of the joy of animal study.

R. M. Lockley
The Private Life of the Rabbit

Before We Begin

Do you know the difference between a cougar, a mountain lion, and a puma? Right you are, there is none. Those are just some of the different names people have given to what is actually one and the same animal. How can that happen? Pretty easily.

Different people in different places at different times have given names to the animals known to them. These "common names" have been handed down from generation to generation, becoming acceptable and comfortable in the cultures where they arose. This process has gone on for centuries among the people of many nations and languages, so it is no wonder some of the names in popular use are occasionally confusing.

In an effort to reduce the confusion and increase understanding, naturalists sort animals into name groups based on the ways in which various creatures are presumed to be related. This can get tricky. Often the obvious differences between animals are not really important, while the real differences are not easy to see. A fish and a whale, for instance, may *look* much alike—the water environment they share has shaped them similarly — but in fact they are very different.

This book is intended to help you understand relationships that may be left unclear by the common names for several very familiar animals.

American crocodile

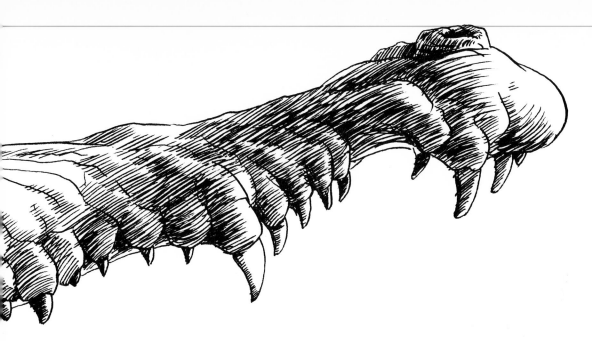

1. Alligator or Crocodile

In fact there are *three* types of animals in the order Crocodilia, not just two. The most easily observed difference among them is the shape of the head.

alligator

Alligators, blunt headed and horny backed, take their name from the Spanish *el lagarto*, "the lizard." Native to China and the Americas, they are said to be slower and clumsier than crocodiles both on land and in water.

Crocodiles also have a thick, bumpy skin, but their heads are longer and narrower than those of alligators. Their name is from the Greek *krokodeilos*, a lizard. Crocodiles are found in Africa, Asia, Australia, and the Americas. They strike very effectively with their strong tails and move rather briskly on land.

Gharials, also called gavials, are the most needle-nosed of crocodilians. Their name, from the Hindi word *ghara*, compares their shape to that of a long-necked water jug. Gharials have somewhat smoother hides than alligators or crocodiles and make their homes in the rivers of India.

Most crocodilians are freshwater animals. Though strong swimmers, they typically inhabit relatively calm, shallow inland waters. Some species may be found in salty coastal water, but there are no true seagoing crocodilians.

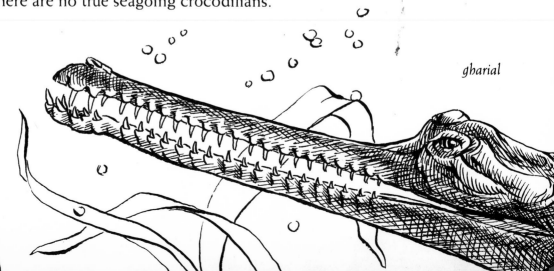

gharial

crocodile

Traditionally naturalists have distinguished among these animals on the basis of teeth. A gharial's teeth are all about the same size. In both alligators and crocodiles, however, the fourth tooth on either side of the lower jaw is exceptionally long. When an alligator closes its mouth, those long teeth slip into sockets in the upper jaw and disappear. When a crocodile closes its mouth, the long teeth remain visible, protruding outside the upper jaw. In general, if you can still see a lot of teeth even when the animal's mouth is closed, you are looking at a crocodile. Alligators have plenty of teeth, but fewer show until the mouth is open.

Like sharks, crocodilians never run out of teeth, for sharp new ones grow in as old dull ones are shed throughout the animals' lives. Numerous as they are, crocodilian teeth serve only for grasping, not chewing. These animals gulp their food in largish chunks and rely on powerful stomach acids to break it down.

Mouth open or closed, no crocodilian can stick out its tongue. In all species the tongue is fixed to the bottom of the mouth along its whole length. This does not render crocodilians silent by any means. The roaring of bull (male) alligators is a sure sign of spring in the swamp. Later come the high-pitched cries of hatchlings.

All crocodilians belong to the very large reptile class of animal life. While other living reptiles have two-chambered hearts, however, crocodilian hearts are four-chambered, like those of birds and mammals.

Crocodilians also belong to the subclass Archosauria ("ruling reptiles"), which dates back over 180 million years and includes the vanished dinosaurs. As far as we know, crocodilians are the only true archosaurs remaining alive today.

As individuals modern crocodilians are the largest of living reptiles. While many never exceed more than a few feet in length, some have been reported at 20 feet (6 meters) or more. None, however, achieve the size common to their prehistoric ancestor *Deinosuchus* ("terror crocodile") of some 70 million years ago, with a skull 6 feet (2 meters) long and an overall length of 49 feet (15 meters). For the "terror crocodile" a dinosaur meant only one thing—dinner.

Any review of crocodilians will bring up the caiman, a name that may have been borrowed from an African Congo dialect. Caiman are native alligators of Central and South America. They can vary from their North American and Chinese cousins in nose shape, body armor, and coloring. One striking example is the black caiman, which is distinctively dark and has especially thick scales.

caiman

Tribes in the Amazon River region called these animals *jacaré*, "floating log." Surely that is one of the most characteristic images of crocodilians, cruising along semisubmerged with only eyes and nose above water. Lacking lips to seal out that water, these animals have two overlapping folds of flesh at the back of the mouth, separating air and food passages. This valve enables them to breathe when the mouth is underwater and only the nostrils are above the surface.

When diving, a crocodilian closes its nose and ears. Like an amphibian, it has a clear inner eyelid, called a nictitating membrane, which covers the eye but allows the animal to see well underwater.

In ancient Egypt and India crocodile worship was common. Dragon gods with crocodilian bodies also appear in the pre-Columbian stonework of Central America and dragon legends in Asian cultures may have begun as stories celebrating encounters between crocodilians and humans.

Given what we know of crocodilian appetites, it is easy to see how humans might find these creatures awesome. Although a typical crocodilian diet emphasizes fish, frogs, water birds, and turtles, these animals are known to eat large mammals—dogs, deer, goats, cattle, and people—when available. Only gharials have no reputation for attacking humans. As a rule, then, take all warning signs very seriously, and if you see a crocodilian coming, get out of its way fast.

All crocodilians favor the warm, wet conditions of tropical or near-tropical climates. They reproduce once yearly, the female coming ashore to lay a clutch of perhaps two to one hundred firm-shelled eggs in a carefully prepared nest. They will guard the nest to some extent during the nine to ten weeks typically needed for the eggs to hatch, and many tend the young for weeks or months after hatching. Ugly or treacherous though they often seem to humans, crocodilians are credited with being the most vigilant of reptile parents. After a year at most, crocodilian hatchlings are ready and able to live entirely on their own; it can be ten years before they in turn are ready to become parents.

Studies of alligator eggs have brought to light the fact that the gender of alligator young depends on the temperature at which the egg is kept in the nest. If the egg stays warm, a male will hatch. If the egg gets cool, the hatchling will be female. This trait, which is also found among some turtles, may help these warm-weather animals adapt their population size— providing more potential egg layers when a drop in temperature seems to signal a challenge to survival.

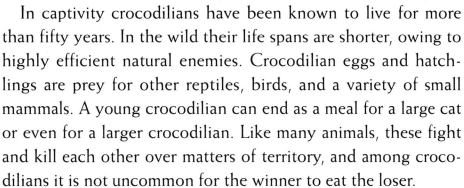

In captivity crocodilians have been known to live for more than fifty years. In the wild their life spans are shorter, owing to highly efficient natural enemies. Crocodilian eggs and hatchlings are prey for other reptiles, birds, and a variety of small mammals. A young crocodilian can end as a meal for a large cat or even for a larger crocodilian. Like many animals, these fight and kill each other over matters of territory, and among crocodilians it is not uncommon for the winner to eat the loser.

For centuries humans regarded crocodilians as dangerous, unlovely, and of little value until safely dead. A brisk trade in their durable, attractively tanned hides led to their near extinction all over the globe. Today crocodilians are raised on farms for their profitable skins, and conservation efforts are seeking to protect the wild populations.

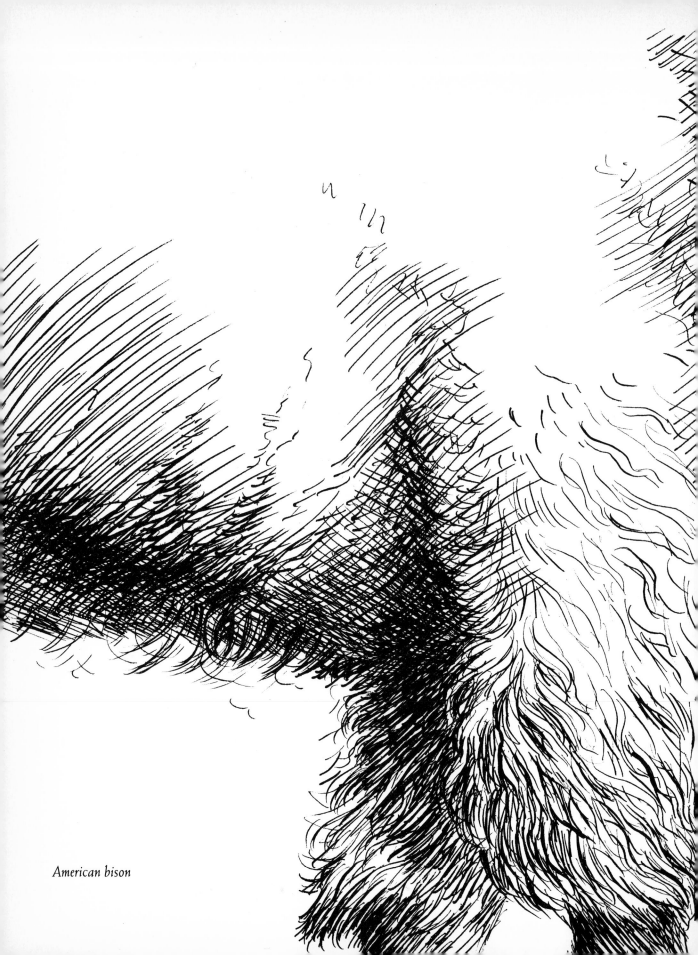

American bison

2. <u>Bison or Buffalo</u>

Especially in North America the terms "bison" and "buffalo" have sometimes been used as if both meant the same thing. Actually, these are different animals.

wisent

The animal native to the plains country of North America and the forests of northern Europe is the bison. Presently two species are recognized.

All bison are herbivores (plant eaters). In keeping with its woodsy origins, the European bison, or wisent, prefers a diet of leaves, twigs, and bark, while the American bison usually dines on grass. The European bison may look lighter than its American cousin, especially around the head and neck. It has longer legs and a less pronounced hump of muscle over the shoulders than is characteristic of the American bison. Both animals are brownish in color and develop heavy coats for winter, which they shed in spring. Their horns are typically short, perhaps 2 feet (60 centimeters) long, and wideset.

American bison

Bison are massive animals, standing an average of 6 feet (2 meters) at the shoulder and often weighing as much as 2,000 pounds (900 kilograms). Despite their bulk, once in motion herds of bison have been clocked at the impressive speed of 30 miles (50 kilometers) per hour.

A female bison requires nine months to produce a calf she will nurse for at least six months. Calves are young adults at two to three years of age, and a total life span of twenty-five years is average.

Buffalo are the animals native to Asia and Africa. Some six species are recognized, including dwarf varieties. Buffalo are externally different from bison and internally different as well—bison have 14 pairs of ribs, buffalo have 13. Darker and less shaggy than bison, buffalo are most commonly about 5 feet (1.5 meters) tall at the shoulder. At that height they average a weight of around 1,700 pounds (800 kilograms); males are typically taller and heavier than females. Buffalo can also have large, impressively curving horns that may exceed a length of 4 feet (1.2 meters)—sharp, serious weapons.

Cape buffalo

A female buffalo produces a single calf after a pregnancy of nine to eleven months. Calves are nursed for six to nine months and become young adults at about three years of age. Twenty years is an average life span. All buffalo are grass grazers, and all buffalo love to wallow in water, or on occasion mud, which helps rid them of insect pests.

African cape buffalo are wild animals capable of defending themselves and each other against the big cats, such as lions, that are their natural enemies. There are some wild water buffalo, called arna, but the greatest numbers are tame farm animals. These are prized throughout the world for their strength, gentleness, and high production of especially rich milk, from which yogurt was originally derived.

The word *bison* is Latin but seems to have originated as *wisunt* among the Germanic tribes of northern Europe. The term buffalo is from the Greek *bubalos*, first applied to wild oxen.

Bison and buffalo are bovid (oxlike) mammals of the Artiodactyla (even-toed) order and belong to the suborder Ruminantia (cud chewers). Their fossil record begins only about 25 million years ago with a deer-sized ancestor dubbed *Eotragus*.

Eotragus

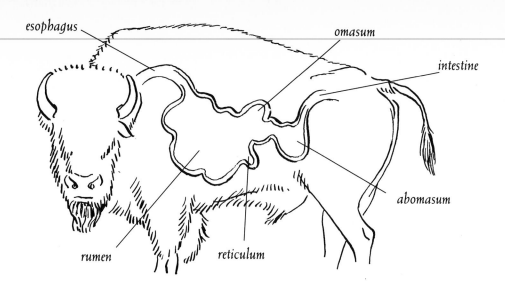

esophagus · omasum · intestine · abomasum · rumen · reticulum

There are a lot of ruminants in the world today, among them antelope, cattle, giraffes, and sheep as well as bison and buffalo. All ruminants are equipped with what is called a "complex" stomach. The "simple" human stomach is just a sort of fleshy bag. The more elaborate ruminant stomach has pockets. As it grazes, a ruminant passes half-chewed food into one of its stomach compartments, called the rumen, where it is broken down by digestive juices. Later the food is returned to the mouth, to be chewed a second time before being swallowed permanently into a series of three more chambers, the reticulum, the omasum, and the abomasum. The chambered stomach permits a ruminant to collect food for slightly later use.

Thousands of years ago buffalo were domesticated, meaning they were tamed and then bred specifically to serve humans. As a result they are common today, particularly in Europe and Asia. One estimate put the world population of water buffalo at 75 million, with 50 million of those in India and Pakistan. They have been introduced into Hawaii, Japan, and South America as well as Australia. Brought by early settlers, the buffalo in Australia were simply turned loose when no longer needed by their human owners. With no large natural enemies about, they multiplied rapidly and became wild.

In Africa and Asia human expansion has reduced the land area available to the wild buffalo, and their numbers are small. The effect of competition with humans is even more drastic in the history of the bison.

Vast bison herds once roamed North America from Canada to Mexico and played an important role in the life of Native American tribes. Settlers began eliminating the bison during westward expansion, a process that reached its peak as railroad building advanced across the continent. By 1889 it was estimated that only 1,000 bison remained, some 800 in captivity, perhaps 200 in the wild. In 1905 the American Bison Society was founded in New York. In 1907 the Canadian government moved the largest surviving herd onto a reservation. Since then numbers of the American animal have increased.

Less frequently dramatized yet every bit as relentless was the bison extermination in Europe, where enormous herds once ranged from Spain to Russia. Despite widespread awareness that the wisent was in jeopardy by the eighteenth century, people continued to hunt the animals until the early 1920s, when the last known wild one was killed. In 1923 the International Society for the Preservation of the European Bison was founded in Berlin. After that, measures were taken to rebuild herds from the fewer than seventy animals that remained.

All bison on both continents now survive in zoos or managed herds.

Bactrian camel

3. Camel or Dromedary

There really is no camel-*or*-dromedary question. There are two types of camel. Each has its own hump structure and native range. Otherwise there is not much difference between them.

Arabian camel

The word camel may stem from the Arab verb *jamala*, meaning "to bear" or "to carry."

The animal with one hump is the Arabian camel, relied upon for thousands of years throughout North Africa and the Middle East. This is the animal also referred to as a dromedary. That name comes from Greek words meaning "to run" or "racecourse."

The camel with two humps is the Asian member of the family, the Bactrian camel. That name arose because the animal was once (mistakenly) believed to have originated in the ancient kingdom of Bactria, an area now known as the Balkh district of northern Afghanistan.

The Bactrian camel is a little stockier in build than the Arabian. The Bactrian averages about 7 feet (2.1 meters) tall at the hump and weighs about 1,800 pounds (815 kilograms). The Arabian camel generally stands 7.5 feet (2.2 meters) at the hump and weighs around 1,600 pounds (725 kilograms).

Bactrian camel

Both types of camel produce a single colt after a pregnancy of about a year. The baby stays with its mother for two years and is considered a young adult at age five. Total average life span for any camel is about twenty to thirty years.

Both types of camel have bushy eyebrows and double, interlocking rows of eyelashes as well as the ability to close their nostrils. This is all for protection against blowing snow or sand. Both types are herbivorous and have cleft (split) upper lips similar to those of rabbits. They also have very tough mouths, enabling them to graze on thorny desert plants.

Both types also have wide, thickly padded feet and can walk well on sand or snow.

Of course, both are also famous for being able to do without fresh food or water for long periods of time.

Within its trademark hump or humps, a camel stores about 80 pounds (36 kilograms) of fat. This the animal can convert to nutrition when fresh food is in short supply. The hump shrivels as the fat is used.

Water is not so much stored by the camel's fur-insulated body as it is conserved. When water is available, a camel can easily drink 15 gallons (57 liters) at once. The camel will retain that water more efficiently than many other mammals because a camel passes off very little water in the form of perspiration or waste. Able to transport loads of 400 pounds (180 kilograms) an average of 40 miles (64 kilometers) a day, a camel may travel a hundred hot, desert miles (160 kilometers) before needing fresh water.

The Bactrian camel was probably domesticated about four thousand years ago. A few wild herds are said to remain in the deserts of Asia.

camel's "cushioned foot"

The Arabian camel began serving humans perhaps six thousand years ago. The Bible's Book of Genesis makes several references to camels in the story of Abraham, indicating that the animals have long been an important part of Middle East life. Baggage camels carried cargo, while the lighter, faster racing camels transported only riders and could cover as much as 100 miles (160 kilometers) in a day.

Because camels can function so well in barren country, early explorers took them to Australia. When the animals were no longer needed, they, like the buffalo, were turned loose to forage for themselves. Without any large predators to threaten them, the camels multiplied. Today there are thousands of them, some in wild herds, some on ranches. The Alice Springs Camel Cup Race is a very popular annual event in Australia.

Camels are among very many kinds of animals in the Artiodactyla order. The camelid family is, however, the only known one surviving in the suborder Tylopoda ("cushioned foot").

llama

At one time there were several families of tylopods on earth and North America was home to quite a large variety of camelids. These included *Poebrotherium*, which was smaller than today's average sheep. Some 2 million years ago large numbers of animals, including the camel ancestors, migrated out of North America to take up residence elsewhere. After that time the fossil record finds *Camelus*, the true camels, in Eurasia. The family emerged in South America as the handsome, surefooted llamas of the Andean mountain regions.

Llamas are the only other surviving camelids known. They include the wild species of vicuña and guanaco and the domestic llama and alpaca. Smaller than camels, all llamas have shortish tails and lack a hump. With straighter necks and taller ears, llamas have a more alert and graceful look than their camel cousins. Nevertheless, llamas share the family trait of great stamina and have served humans as pack animals for thousands of years. The alpaca and vicuña are prized for their very fine wool.

In general, camels are notorious for bad breath, bad temper, and a bad bite. In the German language *Kamel* was once a slang word meaning a stupid person. In seventeenth-century England *camell* meant an "awkward, hulking fellow." Llamas are known to lay back their ears and spit when frightened or provoked, but they are not so widely ill-reputed for it.

Though once indispensable to human survival in many parts of the world, camels are gradually being displaced. For light and heavy hauling across rugged terrain, humans increasingly prefer to rely on cars and trucks. In South America, llamas continue to be valuable herd animals, but their natural range is greatly reduced.

vicuña   *alpaca*   *guanaco*

white-tailed jackrabbit

4. <u>Ha</u>re or <u>R</u>abbit

Hares and rabbits are a couple of animal cousins easily mistaken for one another.

hare

rabbit

Generally hares are larger than rabbits, averaging 2 feet (60 centimeters) long and weighing from 3 to 12 pounds (1 to 5 kilograms). Hares have longer legs than rabbits, longer (often black-tipped) ears, and longer tails. Even so, in North America hares are often referred to as jack*rabbits*.

The animals collectively known as true rabbits include the European or Old World wild rabbits, smaller and plumper than hares. All breeds of domestic rabbit are believed to be descended from these and are identified as members of the Old World wild rabbit species. Widespread throughout North America are several other species of true rabbit commonly called cottontails.

The popular European domestic rabbit breed called the Belgian *hare* is an often-cited example of the name confusion found among these animals.

rabbit kittens (above) and hare leverets, a few days old

The differences between rabbits and hares are particularly evident when the animals are very young.

A newborn hare, called a leveret, is fully furred, open eyed, and equipped with teeth. It is able to run shortly after birth. The leveret will be nursed for about two weeks. Hares are not especially devoted parents. Their young are born above ground and receive minimal care.

In contrast the young of wild rabbits, called kittens, are born naked, blind, deaf, and toothless. The mother rabbit conceals them underground in a specially prepared burrow nest, from which they only begin to emerge after about twenty days.

Hares are solitary aboveground dwellers. They shelter beneath rocks or may take over another animal's abandoned den. Some will scratch out a shallow area called a form, but that is the extent of their "housebuilding." Special glands on a hare's head emit a scent, which it rubs off on twigs, rocks, and grass to mark its territory. If danger threatens, a hare relies on a burst of its famous speed for escape. Over relatively short distances, hares have been clocked at 40 miles (64 kilometers) per hour.

Rabbits are social animals and live together in systems of connecting tunnels called warrens. For these underground burrows they usually select woodlands or brushy clumps, where their homes will be well concealed. Lacking the speed of a hare, a frightened rabbit may briefly "freeze" in place, then duck into one of those handy tunnels.

Both hares and rabbits gain a measure of protection from fur color that blends with their typical surroundings. Some, like the North American snowshoe hares, will shed speckled summer coats and take on a snowy winter white.

Both rabbits and hares belong to the Leporidae family (from Latin, *lepor* for "hare"; *idae*, "like") of the Lagomorpha order (from Greek, *lagos* for "hare"; *morph*, "form"). Both types of animal share the features of a split upper lip and strongly haunched rear legs, longer than the two front legs, which make possible their characteristic hop or leap.

At one time hares and rabbits were classified as rodents. Like squirrels, mice, hamsters, and such, their enlarged front teeth, called incisors, grow all their lives and must be kept worn down by continuous gnawing. Eventually naturalists recognized the differences between lagomorphs and rodents. In general, lagomorphs have larger ears and shorter tails than rodents, and only the lagomorphs have a double row of upper front teeth.

Lagomorphs are believed to have originated in Asia perhaps 50 to 60 million years ago. *Palaeolagus* is an early fossil form.

hare skull

rodent skull

double row of incisors

31

Both hares and rabbits are typically nocturnal (active by night), staying undercover most of the day. They are also voracious herbivores, capable of munching up a lot of vegetation, including human food crops. In turn they are preyed upon by just about every carnivore (meat eater) there is: wolves, foxes, all kinds of cats, large birds, and people, to name only the best known. In captivity hares and rabbits can live five to seven years; in the wild the average drops to a little more than a year.

Despite short life spans, most types of rabbits and hares are in no danger of becoming extinct. One reason is their well-known reproductive ability. Just one mating pair can produce as many as four litters in a year, each litter consisting of up to eight or ten young. Depending on the species, those young may be only four to eight months old when they start producing litters.

Because they reproduce quickly and in great numbers, and consume so much vegetation, rabbits and hares have often become a nuisance. During the nineteenth century, for purposes of sport hunting, humans brought the animals to Australia and South America, where they did not occur naturally. They soon became serious pests on both continents.

New Zealand

English lop ear

Domestication is another good reason for the abundance of rabbits. Thousands of years ago people began keeping and raising these animals for their nutritious meat and useful fur. It is estimated that today there are more than fifty domestic breeds in literally hundreds of varieties. Among the most familiar are the pink-eyed New Zealand and the top-heavy-looking English lop ear. Domestic rabbits range in size from the Netherland dwarf rabbit, at a total weight of perhaps 2 pounds (1 kilogram) up to the Flemish giant at 17 to 20 pounds (7 to 9 kilograms).

Netherland dwarf

Flemish giant

antelope jackrabbit

Sumatran short-eared rabbit

Largest known of the wild cousins is the American hare called the antelope jackrabbit, with a body length of about 27 inches (70 centimeters). This animal is renowned for its exceptionally tall ears and its ability to jump great distances.

The rare and very striking little Sumatran short-eared rabbit is believed to be the only wild cousin with a striped coat.

Though hares and rabbits are chiefly silent animals, some are known to "purr" if annoyed, and they may emit a piercing cry when very frightened. There is another family in the Lagomorph order, however—the Ochotonidae (from *ochodona*, the name originally given them by the Mongol Tatars)—and *they* are regular little chatterboxes.

pika

Native to the great mountain ranges of Asia and North America, these "singing lagomorphs" are the short-haired, short-eared, short-legged wild pikas (from *piika*, their name in a Siberian dialect). Pikas are unlike other lagomorphs in life-style as well as in appearance.

For one thing, these small animals are diurnal (active by day), retreating to burrows or rocky dens at night. Also unlike their longer-eared relatives, the members of pika colonies are very vocal. Sometimes singly, sometimes in choruses, pikas use a whole vocabulary of calls to communicate with one another. This trait earned them an English-language nickname, "whistling hare."

The herbivorous pikas store food for later use, and some will even lay the food out to dry before storing it. The Russians named them "haystack makers" for this food-gathering style. Also, a pika's front and back legs are about equal in length, so these animals run rather than hop. Pikas are the smallest lagomorphs, averaging 6 to 12 inches (15 to 30 centimeters) long and weighing as little as 3.5 ounces (100 grams).

Because the natural range of wild pikas is rather narrow and remote, most people seldom encounter these shy creatures. So if you are going to the Himalayas or the Rockies and can quietly observe a wild pika, a record of your experience would make a terrific science report.

common octopus

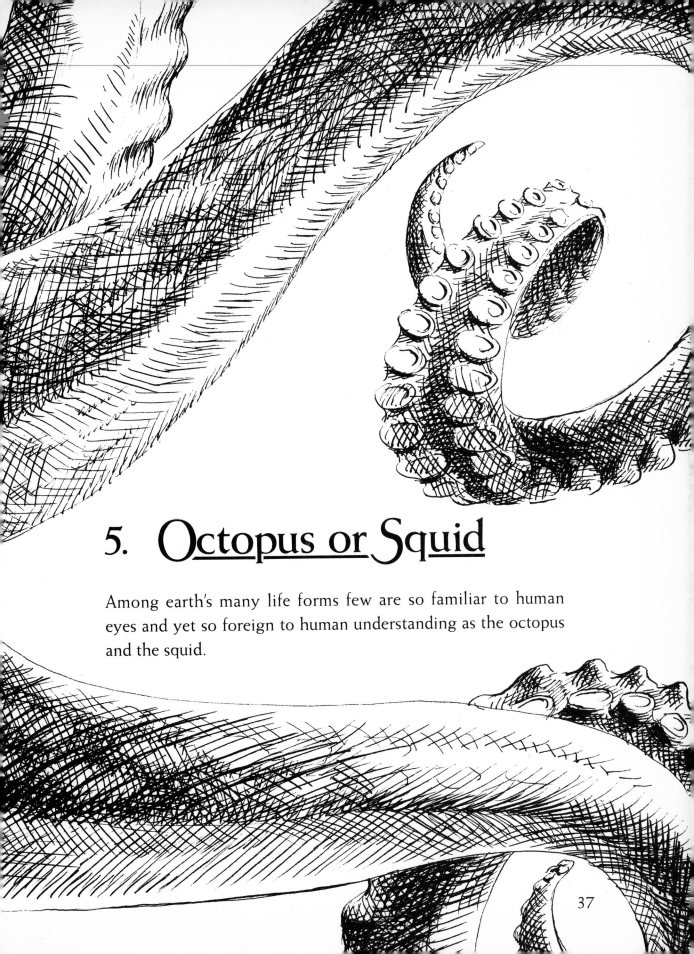

5. Octopus or Squid

Among earth's many life forms few are so familiar to human eyes and yet so foreign to human understanding as the octopus and the squid.

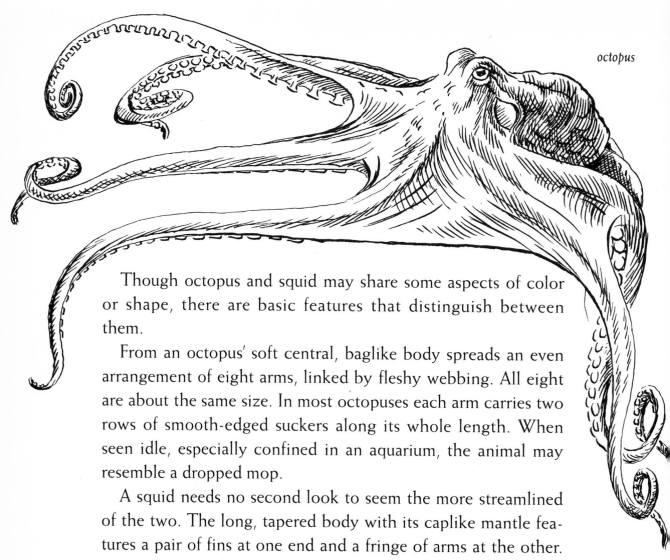

octopus

Though octopus and squid may share some aspects of color or shape, there are basic features that distinguish between them.

From an octopus' soft central, baglike body spreads an even arrangement of eight arms, linked by fleshy webbing. All eight are about the same size. In most octopuses each arm carries two rows of smooth-edged suckers along its whole length. When seen idle, especially confined in an aquarium, the animal may resemble a dropped mop.

A squid needs no second look to seem the more streamlined of the two. The long, tapered body with its caplike mantle features a pair of fins at one end and a fringe of arms at the other. A squid, however, has eight arms that are about equal in size and two clearly longer than the rest, for a total of ten. The longer pair, called tentacles, typically have suckers only on the flattened tips. A squid's suckers usually have hooked or toothed edges.

squid

38

Octopus and squid belong to the class of animal life called Cephalopoda. This is from Greek words meaning "head foot," and at first glance a cephalopod does not seem to consist of much else. Within the body sac, however, both octopus and squid have organs common among animals on earth. Each has a stomach, liver, kidneys—and three hearts. One heart pumps the blue-green blood, which takes its color from a high copper content. Unlike the iron in red human blood, copper is not very efficient for carrying oxygen, so the other two hearts work constantly with the animal's gills to draw needed oxygen from the water.

A cephalopod can "sniff" its surroundings through what are called olfactory organs located near the eyes. The animal also has powerful jaws forming a sharp, beakish mouth and a particularly rough-surfaced tongue, called a radula, for crunching shellfish and other prey. A strong substance produced by glands in the mouth helps render that prey immobile and aids digestion by breaking the food down into an easily swallowed liquid.

Cephalopods are noted for large, well-developed eyes, which have many features in common with the complex eyes of mammals. Cephalopod vision is believed to be very good. These animals also have considerable learning ability. The octopus in particular has demonstrated a capacity for recognition, recall, and even some problem solving that has surprised many researchers.

octopus's eye

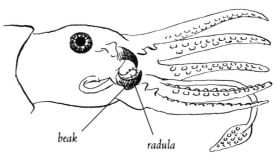

beak radula

cutaway view of squid

39

In the open sea most cephalopods can surprise predators by producing a cloud of dark fluid when threatened. Under that cover they try to escape quickly by means of jet action. The jet is achieved by a series of muscle contractions forcing water through a tube visible at one side of the body above the arms. For further concealment many of these animals have the handy ability to change color—and, in the case of the octopus, even to take on the texture of the surrounding surface. The result is that they can become just about invisible. These abilities are their defense against the many sea mammals, fish, and birds that find cephalopods a highly nourishing diet. Octopus and squid are also enjoyed as human food in many parts of the world.

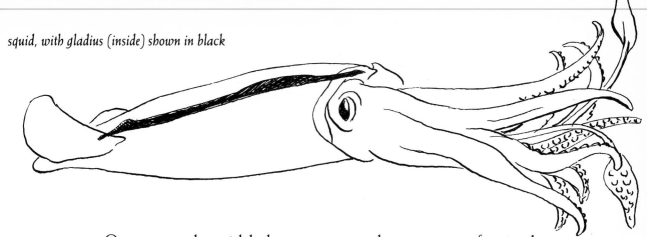

squid, with gladius (inside) shown in black

Octopus and squid belong to a very large group of animals termed mollusks, from the Latin *mollis*, meaning soft. Certainly that describes the bodies of most cephalopods. Within a squid there is one long, slender, firm structure called a gladius, which supports the flesh. Lacking even that, an octopus is so soft and flexible, it can compress itself to vanish through an opening said to be hardly bigger than the animal's own eye.

Most mollusks—which include snails and oysters—protect themselves by creating a living outer shell, built up in layers from a calcium carbonate material produced in their bodies. When the animal dies, the shell often remains. Shells have been found in fossil beds dating back more than 500 million years.

Once there were many cephalopods with shells. The only known remaining type is the nautilus. Fringed with about a hundred short, smooth arms, the nautilus gets around by jetting water through the chambers of its shell and has no ink sac.

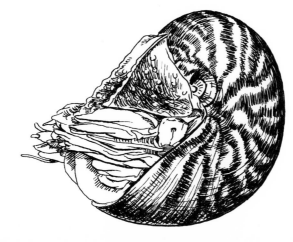

nautilus

41

cuttlefish

Today's cephalopods are marine (saltwater) animals found throughout the oceans of the world. In addition to the nautilus they include the family of cuttlefish. On average cuttlefish are only 1 to 35 inches (2.5 to 90 centimeters) long and have a pair of narrow fins running the length of the body, one at either side. Capped by a mantle and trailing a pair of retractable tentacles, the cuttlefish may resemble a squid. Inside, however, a cuttlefish has a proportionately large bony central structure that is uncommon among cephalopods. This is called "cuttlebone" and is sold in pet shops as a mineral supplement for the diet of caged birds.

At the other size extreme are the giant squids. Estimated at lengths of 60 feet (18 meters) and more, these are believed to be the world's largest living mollusks. They are preyed upon by sperm whales. Giant squids usually live at great depths in the ocean. Rare sightings of these animals may have given rise to the ancient Norwegian legend of the kraken, a many-armed sea monster.

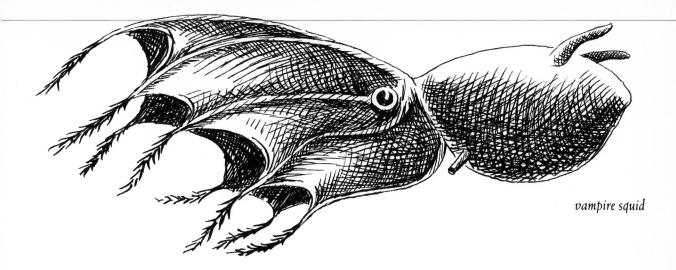

vampire squid

    While most cephalopods do not come even close to the size of a giant squid, the North Pacific octopus has been reported with an arm spread of some 30 feet (9 meters).

    An especially significant cephalopod family is that comprised of just one species, the small, deep-living creatures with big red eyes called vampire squids. These unique animals have fins similar to those of a squid and smooth suckers like an octopus. Lacking ink sacs for defense, vampire squids will conceal themselves within the folds of their own dark mantles, a trait that may have contributed to their horrific name.

    Interesting for other reasons are the arrow squids, some "flying" relatives. To escape predators, arrow squids can use their jet ability with such force that they propel themselves entirely out of the water, skimming the surface and sometimes even landing on the deck of a passing ship.

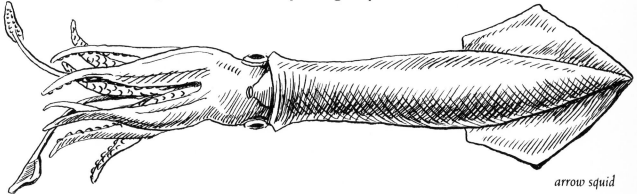

arrow squid

Particularly beautiful are the blue-ringed octopuses of Australia. Quite small and very pretty to look at, these have been called the most dangerous cephalopods in the world. Equipped with two potent toxins, their bite can be fatal to humans. This is one animal you should be sure to avoid.

The young of both octopus and squid come into the world as small, soft, jelly-coated eggs. Most often the female anchors them to a sturdy surface where they remain while the young inside develop.

Squid parents leave their eggs, but the octopus mother stays with hers and actively guards them until they hatch, even if she gives up her own life in the process. Depending on the type of squid or octopus, the spawn may number from a few dozen to several thousand. The hatching time and development pattern of the young also vary with the particular type of animal. Averages of cephalopod life span run from one year to as many as ten; the larger animals living in deeper water are believed to be the longest lived.

Squids tend to be gregarious animals. They school together and are often found jetting about the seas in groups of thousands. The octopus prefers a solitary life. Joining its own kind only to mate, the octopus will then return to the privacy of its den, a refuge to which it will cling tenaciously.

Though many people consider cephalopods repulsive, researchers who have worked with octopuses in the lab or ocean describe them otherwise. Spoken of as shy and flower-like, the octopus is also said to be bright and readily tamed.

For its part, the squid has served to aid advances in human medicine. The components of a squid's nervous system are so large that responses are especially easy to measure. This has made the animals ideal for study by researchers seeking to overcome disorders such as multiple sclerosis.

California sea lion

6. Seal or Sea Lion

Though very similar, true seals and sea lions are in separate families. Both are carnivorous, aquatic mammals, members of the suborder Pinnipedia. From the Latin *pinna* ("feather") and *ped* ("foot"), the name obviously reflects someone's impression of flippered feet, a trait seals and sea lions share.

47

sea lion

true seal

Of the two, earless true seals are those most streamlined for an aquatic life. The "trained seals" found taking bows at the circus are sea lions, those best suited to show business.

True seals belong to the Phocidae family (from Latin *phoca*, "seal"). They have short necks and no visible external ears. Their hind limbs are used only for swimming and are dragged when the animal is on land. A true seal's front flippers are furred and clawed and are held against the body when the seal is swimming.

Sea lions are in the Otariidae family (from Latin *otaria*, "ear"). Longer-necked, they have small visible ears and use their hind limbs as legs for walking on land. A sea lion's forelimbs have no fur or claws and the animal paddles with them when swimming.

The eared sea lion family includes several pinniped species collectively known by the common name "fur seals." To distinguish fur seals from the earless true seals, look for the clearly visible little tab ears; luxurious coats set fur seals apart from their short-haired sea lion cousins.

There are more than thirty species of pinnipeds. Though details of coloring and life-style vary among them, it can be said that most select a diet of fish, shellfish, and cephalopods. Pinnipeds in turn are regular fare for such big eaters as sharks, polar bears, and some whales. Even so, studies indicate pinnipeds can average life spans of twelve to thirty years in the wild.

On land even the most agile sea lion is at a disadvantage. In human terms, these animals walk on their ankles and wrists, which is not very fast or very graceful. Once in water, though, the streamlined pinniped is a powerful, elegant swimmer.

Pinnipeds are called pelagic animals, meaning they live at sea. Indeed, except in the mating and pupping seasons, pinnipeds are most often found in the ocean, swimming or diving. Field studies have discovered that some of these animals dive far deeper than had been previously realized. One expedition reported elephant seals averaging forty-three dives in two hours, some to depths gauged at more than 3,000 feet (900 meters). Even with elaborate diving gear humans cannot do the same.

Thick layers of fat called blubber insulate pinnipeds against heat loss in water. The animal can use this blubber as nutrition when fresh food is scarce. When pinnipeds come ashore to produce and tend their babies, thick, hairy coats protect them from heat loss in the cold air.

Mediterranean monk seal

harp seal pup

Pinniped females are known to be subject to "delayed reproduction." In most mammals as soon as an egg has been fertilized, an infant begins to develop. In pinnipeds a fertilized egg can float within the mother for several months. With the approach of pupping season, the egg attaches and a baby seal begins to take shape.

Most often just one pup is born. Pups arrive well developed, fully furred, often with their eyes open, and able to swim. Some infant seals have fluffy white coats that blend with the snow or ice where they are born. As the animal gets older, the coat darkens.

Surely one of the most instantly endearing animal infants anywhere is a big-eyed seal pup, but do not let that baby face mislead you; keep your fingers in your pockets. Like its mom and dad, the pup has a healthy set of teeth and is capable of a bone-shattering bite, even if it was only meant in play.

A pinniped mother's milk is very rich, and the baby grows quickly. Exactly how long the pup is nursed and remains with its mother depends on the specific type of animal—and there are some fascinating types.

Ringed seals are named for their distinctive coats, though markings can vary among them. These include several varieties of freshwater seals found in the lakes of Finland and Russia.

ringed seal

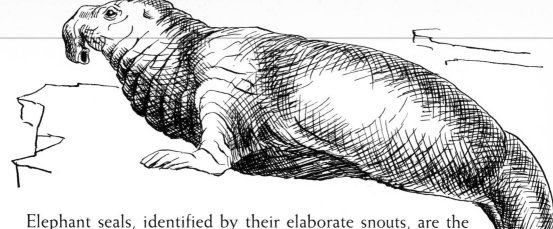

Elephant seals, identified by their elaborate snouts, are the largest pinnipeds on earth. Native to the cold waters of both northern and southern hemispheres, they have been reported at sizes up to 20 feet (6 meters) long and weights of 8,800 pounds (4,000 kilograms).

leopard seal

Antarctic leopard seals are noted for spots and an aggressive disposition. They regularly prey on warm-blooded animals such as penguins and other seals.

Among the Steller's sea lions of the northern Pacific and their cousins the southern sea lions, males wear a tawny "mane" in keeping with their name.

Steller's sea lion

There is a third pinniped family, the Odobenidae (from Greek, "tooth walker"), better known as walruses. As is also true among elephants, walruses' trademark tusks are grown by both males and females. Walrus tusks reach lengths of 3 feet (1 meter). Walruses average a body size of 10 to 12 feet (3 to 4 meters) long and typically weigh about 3,000 pounds (1,360 kilograms). They prefer shallow water and spend more time on the beach than other pinnipeds, occasionally using those impressive tusks to haul themselves ashore.

The fossil record of pinnipeds goes back about 20 million years and includes the ancestral *Enaliarctidae*. Pinnipeds are believed to have first emerged in the North Pacific, where so many of them are still at home. Eventually they found habitats in both the north and south polar regions as well as in between. The warm-water cousins are the monk seals—the Hawaiian monk seal, Caribbean monk seal, and Mediterranean monk seal. These have become the rarest of all pinnipeds. The Caribbean animal is believed to be already extinct.

The threat of extinction is not new for pinnipeds. Their fur, their oil, their meat, and their ivory have all been valued by humans, who have killed them in great numbers for centuries. Curbing the trade in such goods as the white fur of baby seals has helped, but pinnipeds continue to be at risk from pollutants in the oceans. Where conservation efforts have been in place for a while, they appear to be working, and naturalists are still able to study these animals in their own element, the sea.

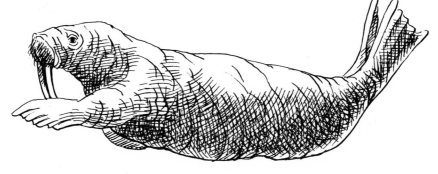

desert tortoise

7. <u>Tortoise or Turtle</u>

Surely these reptiles in shells are among the most instantly recognizable animals in the world. Once you have seen a turtle you will never mistake one for anything else, except maybe another turtle.

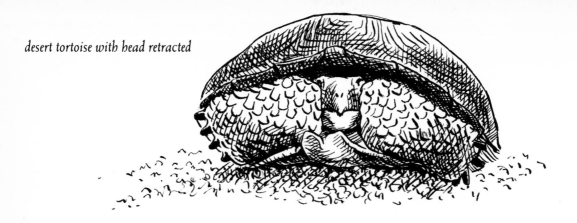

desert tortoise with head retracted

There are different life-style groups among turtles and over time these led to different common names for various animals.

Terrapin is a North American name (from *torope*, "little turtle" in the Algonquin language) for freshwater turtles caught for food. One of these is the diamondback terrapin which, despite the implication of its common name, prefers to live in salty coastal waters.

Tortoise (from Latin *tortus*, "twisted," apparently a reference to the turned look of the animals' feet) designates terrestrial (land-dwelling) turtles. These include Aesop's storybook racing hero as well as the real-life Galapagos tortoises, some of which weigh more than 500 pounds (227 kilograms).

Turtle (also from *tortus*) is the correct general term for all of earth's living shelled reptiles. Along with the terrapins and tortoises, these include such ocean-dwelling cousins as the hawksbill sea turtle. For decades this animal was aggressively hunted for its beautiful shell which, in human hands, was misleadingly referred to as "tortoiseshell."

hawksbill sea turtle

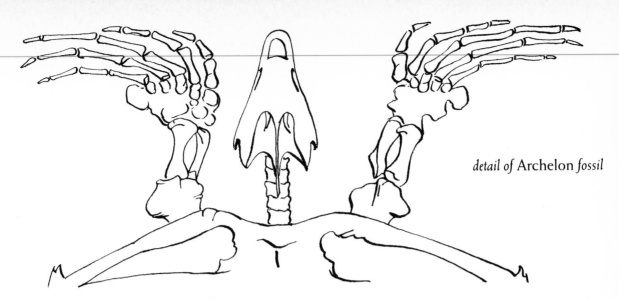

detail of Archelon *fossil*

Turtles have trod their patient way across earth for some 200 million years. Members of the reptile class, they appear to be the only living members of the ancient suborder Anapsida. From the Greek, *anapsid* means "without arch" and refers to the distinctive shape of a turtle's head. All reptile ancestors are believed to have been anapsids, but while many reptile families changed throughout the eons, turtles have remained remarkably the same. Paddling about in the world's oceans 100 million years ago was *Archelon*, known to us only as a fossil. At 12 feet (3.6 meters) wide, flipper to flipper, this animal was enormous yet unmistakably a turtle.

In our own time turtles do not grow to that size, but they exist in splendid diversity.

Big-headed turtles of Asia do not retract their heads into their shells. Instead each has a little "helmet" of bone for protection.

big-headed turtle

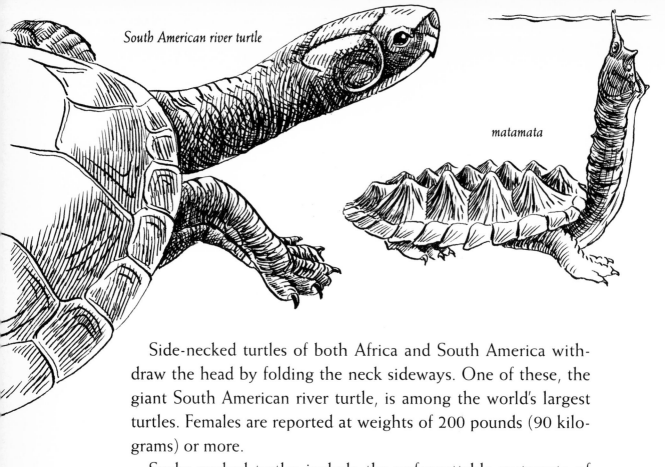

South American river turtle

matamata

Side-necked turtles of both Africa and South America withdraw the head by folding the neck sideways. One of these, the giant South American river turtle, is among the world's largest turtles. Females are reported at weights of 200 pounds (90 kilograms) or more.

Snake-necked turtles include the unforgettable matamata of Brazil, whose strange appearance serves as camouflage.

Softshell turtles include the big-eyed Malayan, with its funnellike nose and flattened shape.

There are beautiful turtles such as the star tortoise of India with its handsomely marked domed shell.

Malayan turtle

star tortoise

alligator snapping turtle

And there are ugly turtles, among which the alligator snapping turtle, native to North America, surely takes the prize. Blending into a cluttered river bottom, it lurks with mouth open, displaying a fleshy knob that unwary fish mistake for a worm. Some of these turtles weigh in at 200 pounds (90 kilograms).

The very largest turtles left on earth are the leatherback sea turtles, named for their smooth shells. Leatherbacks are known to be over 8 feet (2.4 meters) in length and to weigh 1,300 pounds (600 kilograms) or more. They have been found as far north as the Arctic Circle and as far south as New Zealand. The venomous jellyfish seems to be an important part of the leatherback diet.

leatherback sea turtle

59

In any configuration, though, all turtles have basic qualities in common.

Plain or fancy, hard or soft, every turtle has a living, growing shell. The shell consists of the carapace on top and the plastron underneath, which may be joined at the sides by sections called bridges. Aquatic turtles often bask in the sun, not only to regulate body temperature but also to produce the vitamins needed for a healthy shell. That shell is a sturdy shield protecting and identifying the turtle inside.

Lacking teeth, most types of turtle today have a beaked snout for ripping vegetation or gripping prey. Once seized, a turtle's meal—be it fish, frog, fruit, carrion, worm, insect, or leafy green—is chomped until the pieces become small enough to swallow. Turtles can also store reserves of fat for nourishment when fresh food is scarce.

box turtle

nostril

beak

ear

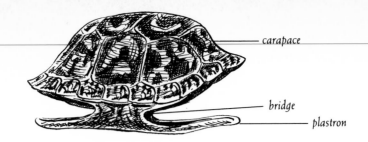

carapace

bridge

plastron

All turtles require water, and those coping with arid environments store it in their bodies for use as needed. Marine turtles are equipped with what are called lachrymal glands near the eyes, through which they pass off excess salt ingested with the seawater.

Though aquatic turtles ordinarily breathe through their noses, they are able to obtain oxygen directly from the water and remain submerged for varying lengths of time. In very cool or very dry climates an ability to get by on minimal oxygen when necessary serves a turtle when it goes underground for a season.

The turtle's reputation for slow motion is well founded. Though aquatic turtles are efficient swimmers, a combination of short legs and heavy shell prevents any of these animals from breaking speed records on land.

A turtle's ponderous pace, however, should not be interpreted as evidence that these animals lack keen awareness of their world. Researchers have determined that turtle vision is very good and that the animals are able to distinguish colors. Turtles also actively respond to odors and to touch. Some researchers credit them with learning ability equal to that of a laboratory rodent. A turtle's hearing, though apparently adequate to the animal's needs, is presently believed confined to a narrow range of rather low sounds. Perhaps this is because a turtle's ear is covered by skin on the outside of the head. And though some turtles are known to emit grunting or roaring calls during the mating season, essentially they are silent creatures.

Even turtles that otherwise spend their whole lives in water reproduce by laying firm-shelled eggs in hidden or buried nests on land. It is known that female turtles can go on laying eggs for more than a year after mating, a trait similar to the delayed reproduction in seals.

Some turtles produce only one clutch of eggs each year, others several. Depending on the type of turtle, there can be from two to two hundred eggs, which generally require two to three months to hatch if conditions of temperature and moisture are right.

Turtles do no parenting at all. The mother prepares a nest, deposits her eggs, and leaves. As the young emerge from the eggs, they must fend for themselves.

It is a dangerous world for turtle eggs and infants. Birds, animals, and humans prey on the eggs. Birds, animals, and fish prey on the hatchlings. Full-grown turtles are at risk from a variety of animals, and also from humans who dine on the flesh and make implements of many kinds from the shells.

Anyone handling turtles should be aware that several species carry bacteria very dangerous to humans. Anytime you touch a turtle, wash your hands thoroughly with warm water and soap before going on to anything else.

Turtles are noted for longevity. While certain claims may be difficult to prove, there is reason to suppose some of these animals have lived for a hundred years. For this capacity, as well as for their distinctive appearance and stately style of locomotion, turtles have been revered in cults around the world. An ancient Chinese belief was that markings on turtle carapaces could foretell the future.

Turtles seem never to have been feared or despised by humans, as so many other reptiles have been. Even so, expanding human populations and spreading pollution endanger turtles and their habitats. Conservation efforts in several countries have only begun to preserve those species considered most at risk.

What's in a Name?

"What's in a name?" wrote William Shakespeare in his famous play *Romeo and Juliet.* "A rose by any other name would smell as sweet." Shakespeare did not mean that names are entirely useless, but that human beings must look beyond simple labels to find what is really important about the world and each other.

In these pages you have seen that while a camel is a camel, a "buffalo" may very well be a bison, and some "rabbits" are actually hares.

Recognizing and respecting the qualities that make each living creature unique requires a lot more than just knowing a name. Making the effort to learn and use the most correct name, however, is certainly a good way to begin.

Glossary of Common and Scientific Names

This book uses the terms by which science classifies and expresses relatedness among living organisms. These terms begin with the most general groupings and work inward, to arrive at the most specific.

You are probably aware that within the very large animal *kingdom* there are several *classes* of life. This volume deals with members of three classes, mammals, reptiles, and cephalopods. A class consists of several *orders*. Within an order there are *families*, within a family there can be any number of *genera*, and within any one genus are many *species*.

To convey singular identity as accurately as possible, humans use Latin, the international language of science, to style *scientific names*. The first word of a scientific name indicates the genus an organism belongs to, followed by one or more words to designate its particular species. Scientific names undergo change as new facts come to light, but they are usually more helpful than common names in clarifying a plant or animal's relationship to the world around it.

Before We Begin

Cougar, mountain lion, puma   *Felis concolor*

1. Alligator or Crocodile

American alligator   *Alligator mississippiensis*
Black caiman   *Melanosuchus niger*
Indian gharial or gavial   *Gavialis gangeticus*
Nile crocodile   *Crocodylus niloticus*

2. Bison or Buffalo

African Cape buffalo   *Syncerus caffer*
American bison   *Bison bison*

Arna	*Bubalus arnee arnee*
European bison or wisent	*Bison bonasus*
Water buffalo	*Bubalus arnee*

3. Camel or Dromedary

Alpaca	*Lama guanacoe f. glama*
Arabian camel	*Camelus dromedarius*
Bactrian camel	*Camelus ferus*
Guanaco	*Lama guanacoe huanacos*
Llama	*Lama guanacoe f. glama*
Vicuña	*Lama vicugna*

4. Hare or Rabbit

Antelope jackrabbit	*Lepus alleni*
Belgian hare: see Domestic rabbit	
Black-tailed jackrabbit	*Lepus californicus*
Domestic rabbit	*Oryctolagus cuniculus*
Eastern or Florida cottontail	*Sylvilagus floridanus*
English lop ear: see Domestic rabbit	
European or brown hare	*Lepus europaeus*
European or Old World wild rabbit	*Oryctolagus cuniculus*
Netherland dwarf rabbit: see Domestic rabbit	
New Zealand pink-eyed rabbit: see Domestic rabbit	
Snowshoe hare	*Lepus americanus*
Steppe pika	*Ochotona pusilla*
Sumatran short-eared rabbit	*Nesolagus netscheri*

5. Octopus or Squid

Arrow squid	*Ommastrephes bartrami*
Blue-ringed octopus	*Hapalochlaena maculosa*

Chambered nautilus	*Nautilus pompilius*
Common cuttlefish	*Sepia officinalis*
Common octopus	*Octopus vulgaris*
Common squid	*Loligo vulgaris*
Giant squid	*Architeuthis dux*
North Pacific octopus	*Octopus dofleini*
Vampire squid	*Vampyroteuthis infernalis*

6. Seal or Sea Lion

California sea lion	*Zalophus californianus*
Caribbean monk seal	*Monachus tropicalis*
Gray seal	*Halichoerus grypus*
Harp seal	*Phoca groenlandica*
Hawaiian monk seal	*Monachus schauinslandi*
Leopard seal	*Hydrurga leptonyx*
Mediterranean monk seal	*Monachus monachus*
Northern fur seal	*Callorhinus ursinus*
Ringed seal	*Phoca hispida*
Southern sea lion	*Otaria byronia*
Southern elephant seal	*Mirounga leonina*
Steller's seal lion	*Eumetopias jubatus*
Walrus	*Odobenus rosmarus*

7. Tortoise or Turtle

Alligator snapping turtle	*Macroclemys temminckii*
Big-headed turtle	*Platysternon megacephalum*
Diamondback terrapin	*Malaclemys terrapin*
Galapagos tortoise	*Geochelone nigrita*
Giant South American river turtle	*Podocnemis expansa*
Hawksbill sea turtle	*Eretmochelys imbricata*
Indian star tortoise	*Geochelone elegans*
Leatherback sea turtle	*Dermochelys coriacea*
Malayan softshell turtle	*Dogania subplana*
Matamata (snake-necked)	*Chelus fimbriatus*

Selected Bibliography

Alderton, David. *Turtles and Tortoises of the World.* New York: Facts on File, 1988.

Bull, James J. "Sonny Side Up—Or Down." *Natural History,* April 1988.

Cousteau, Jacques. *Octopus and Squid: The Soft Intelligence.* Garden City, NY: Doubleday, 1973.

Ernst, Carl H., and Roger W. Barbour. *Turtles of the World.* Washington, DC: Smithsonian Institution Press, 1989.

Gentry, Roger L. "Seals and Their Kin." *National Geographic,* April 1987.

Grzimek, Bernhard. *Grzimek's Animal Life Encyclopedia.* New York: Van Nostrand, 1968–84.

Kemp, Mark. "A Squid for All Seasons." *Discover,* June 1989.

LeBoeuf, Burney J. "Incredible Diving Machines." *Natural History,* February 1989.

National Geographic Society. *National Geographic Book of Mammals.* Washington, DC: National Geographic Society, 1981.

Nesis, Kir N. *Cephalopods of the World.* Neptune City, NJ: TFH, 1987.

Parker, Sybil P., ed. *Grzimek's Encyclopedia of Mammals.* New York: McGraw-Hill, 1990.

————. *Synopsis and Classification of Living Organisms.* New York: McGraw-Hill, 1982.

Pickford, G. E. *Vampyroteuthis infernalis Chun.* Dana Reports Nos. 29 and 32. Copenhagen: Carlsberg Foundation, 1946, 1949.

Pritchard, P. C. H. *Living Turtles of the World.* Neptune City, NJ: TFH, 1967.

Riedman, Marianne. *The Pinnipeds: Seals, Sea Lions, and Walruses.* Berkeley: University of California Press, 1990.

Romer, Alfred Sherwood. *Vertebrate Paleontology.* Chicago: University of Chicago Press, 1966.

Ross, Charles A., ed. *Crocodiles and Alligators.* New York: Facts on File, 1989.

White, Christopher R. "Freshwater Turtles: Designed for Survival." *National Geographic,* January 1986.

INDEX

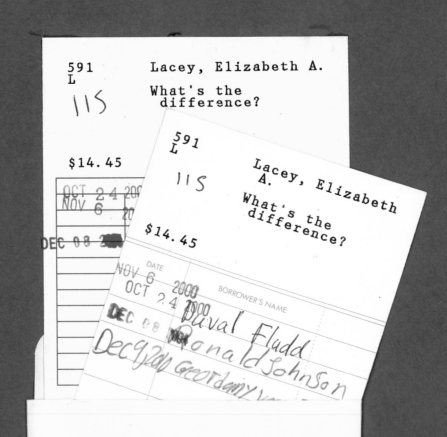

591
L

115

Lacey, Elizabeth A.

What's the
difference?

$14.45

591
L

115

Lacey, Elizabeth
A.

What's the
difference?

$14.45

DATE	BORROWER'S NAME
NOV 6 2000	
OCT 24 2000	Duval Fludd
DEC 08 2000	Ronald Johnson
Dec 9 2000	Geordany